Maybe Today

Also by S.K. Williams
Love by Night

Maybe Today

S.K. Williams

Andrews McMeel
PUBLISHING®

Andrews McMeel Publishing
a division of Andrews McMeel Universal
1130 Walnut Street, Kansas City, Missouri 64106

www.andrewsmcmeel.com

23 24 25 26 27 SDB 10 9 8 7 6 5 4 3 2 1

ISBN: 978-1-5248-7735-4

Library of Congress Control Number: 2022945729

Cover Art and Cover Design by Justin Estcourt

Editor: Patty Rice
Production Designer: Lynn Stoecklein
Production Editor: Brianna Westervelt
Production Manager: Shona Burns

ATTENTION: SCHOOLS AND BUSINESSES
Andrews McMeel books are available at quantity discounts with bulk purchase for educational, business, or sales promotional use. For information, please e-mail the Andrews McMeel Publishing Special Sales Department: sales@amuniversal.com.

for Dad,
I hope you are proud of me

Contents

Prologue

When the two of us met at a bookstore back in 2017, we had no idea that our meeting and our eventual friendship was the start of something so far beyond ourselves.

Writing poetry at the time, for me, was a deeply vulnerable and private exercise. There were a lot of difficult topics, questions, emotions, and experiences that I was working through. Not all of them were coming from a healthy place, but it was always a healthy outlet, to be able to write poetry.

At some point, early in our friendship, we realized we shared a love for poetry. And though the poems I wrote were often very personal, some part of me felt safe to share them with Shayla. It was nerve-racking, handing off that first journal to her, not knowing what her response was going to be.

She read the first journal and gave it back to me the next day, excited to read more. She left sticky notes throughout the journal, identifying pieces that affected her and sharing words of affirmation with me. The next journal I gave her, I told her she could write her thoughts down directly on the page. They were part of the piece now, as far as I was concerned.

Through the next couple years, she began to change my mind about myself. She showed me that there was something valuable I had been missing. I had not been giving myself enough space or time or credit. It all began in those notes, those little annotations.

In our sharing of ideas, thoughts, and later, our feelings, the idea of S.K. Williams blossomed and came to reflect both of us and our journey through life together. Both of our initials are featured in the pseudonym S.K. Williams, which is really a name for the both of us together.

Our hope is that this book reflects the spirit of that relationship, that conversation. There will be hard pages to read, I assure you, but there is also kindness and a beautiful light to guide you, and there is a lot of hope in the end.

We sincerely hope you enjoy this book. It is deeply personal to the two of us.

—Kevin

FALL

Calm

Autumn has always been my favorite season.

There is something about the flaking of frayed
layers, the way the earth peels off her old skin,
a reminder to look back with fondness and
reverence for what has been left behind,
or merely carried on in memory.

The falling away of old leaves,
their somber hues of amber, burnt orange,
and rusty brown, the dreary skies contrasted
with dimly illuminated candlelit desks.

The crisp evening breeze,
wool and knit sweaters abound,
fingers curled out of long sleeves,
pulled in close for weighted comfort.

The weariness and melancholy
are allowed to rest their tired cheeks,
and uncertainty and indecision
give space for reflection and contemplation.

Everything here is gentle and easy,
comforting and reassuring,
a welcome invitation to bundle up inside
and revisit comforting stories,
old days and nights passing into shadow.

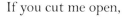

If you cut me open,

You would find only words
wrapped around scars,

Bookshelves
carved out of my bones,

Characters
tiptoeing across my heartstrings,
voyaging through my veins,
and digging deep within me
in search of buried treasure.

They have built a home within me,
welcome refugees
from our cruel world.

Do you know the tender itch
felt by phantom limbs –
the desire to hold
what can never be held again?

Have you ever lost a piece of yourself
you thought would always be there?

If I had a time machine,
I would not go forward, but I would go back.
      To when I was an awkward adolescent
      When I had two parents –
          two functioning, living parents;
      When summer was the world to me
          and every story was full of wonder

Before time nibbled at my rotting limbs,
Before grim contortions overtook my dreams,
Before the flames swelled with my stories,
Before pieces of me began to break away

Now I feel only the longing
to scratch these phantom limbs.

Do you remember
the drive to Dad's house?

The winding road out of town,
weaving between the farmland,
the rancid smell of manure
filling our noses?

Do you remember that burnt shack
we used to pass by, abandoned,
with the yellow tape?

Do you remember Dad used to say one day
he would buy that place and fix it up –
make it into a haunted house?

Do you remember when he would turn on
his signal to pass someone,
but forget to turn it off?

Do you remember passing by Hanford,
the mystery, the allure of the place
where they stored the nuclear bombs?

Do you remember the cha-chunk sounds
as we crossed the big old bridge
and scaled the unrailed mountainside?

Do you remember Saddle Mountain?

Do you remember the town water tower
coming into view on the horizon?

Do you remember
the last time we made that drive together?

Outsider

I'm looking through the frosted glass,
    and on the inside, everyone is doing fine.
    They all have each other.
    They are all smiles and laughs.

On the inside, everything is alright.
    Everyone is safe and warm.
    Everyone in there has a place,
        warming their palms beside the fire,
        sunk back in some plushy couch,
        or sipping some steaming mug of tea.
Everything in there makes sense; it belongs.

I've always been on the outside
                    looking in,
    wanting more than anything else
    to feel understood,
    but I'm not like them, and I never was.

I'm on the outside,
    and it's lonely and sometimes it's cold,
    but I have my journals
        to keep me from going numb.

I've been out here for most of my life
    and some days are easier than others.

But yesterday, it started snowing
    and my journals are starting to get wet.
I just wish they would notice me
    and let me in.
I'm starting to get cold
    and my pages are soaking.
I don't know how much longer
I can stay out here
    before the hypothermia starts to set in.

My white knuckles are rapping on the door
    but they don't seem to hear me
    over the sounds of conversation.
Maybe it's too loud in there
    or maybe the walls are too thick.
Maybe they never even knew I was out here.
Why did they have to lock the door?

I'm calling out to ask for help
    but my yells are drowned
        by the howling wind.

I just want to get in.
Please, just let me in.

Wow, thank you for allowing me to read your journal.
This really resonates with me. I want you to know that I see you —
I hear you. I know how you feel, and you can always come inside my
home, it can be your home too.

Their little jokes,
their crude words,
their whispers to each other,
        puncture holes through my skin.

        Some of it goes over my head,
        but I know when it's about me
        and I know it's never good.

        I hear them now
        even when they're not around.

I wear the armor now
wherever I go.

I will not be caught
with my guard down.

I won't let them get under my skin.

They can call me
whatever they like
but the joke's on them;
I'll never trust again.

Would you ask me what's wrong
        if I don't seem okay?

Would you push me if I lied
        and insisted I'm fine?

And if I was honest with you
        and told you everything inside,

        Would you stay and listen
        or would you leave?

Would you tell me
        if I was falling away from myself?

Would you help me
        remember who I am
                in the gentlest way?

Always, my friend. ♡

Good Kid

Lately I've been thinking
and I don't know what I did wrong.

I turned the other cheek,
but they bruised that one too.

I got the good grades,
I went to bed on time,
I worked hard,
I never asked for anything,
I didn't drink,
I didn't party,
I went to college,
I did everything they told me to do.

Why isn't it working?
Why am I not happy?
When will I be happy?

I'm not better,
I'm just learning
to live with the pain.

Maybe you're not broken,
maybe the world is.

There were good days, too, back then.
    I forget sometimes
        it wasn't all bad.

I don't remember much
    when Mom was still with Dad.

But I remember family walks
    through the neighborhood,
I remember that feeling on the swings –
    it felt so good,
I remember most of the holidays
    and the pizza nights at the arcades,
I remember bouncing on the trampoline
    and my mom's *Reader's Digest* magazines
    and raking leaves in the backyard –
        boy, it was so hard,
I remember the tree in the back
    that we climbed up to look at the sky,
I remember when I got so scared
    that I couldn't come back down,
I remember the corner store
    we would get candy from
        back when a quarter
            could get you some gum.

I miss the good days.

I see myself
in all the places I left behind,
the moments I have forgotten,
the people I don't talk to anymore.

Because they have all come
and passed.

But some of them left footprints
on my skin,
soft like snowflakes,
slowly fading in time.

Some left scars
that will take my whole life
to heal.

They are all gone,
but I am still right here.

It's pretty amazing (for better or worse) how people
can imprint themselves on us. And how we can do
that to others too.

I miss how close we used to be,
 how late we would stay up,
 talking about the world,
 staring off into the sky,
 with the stars around us spinning by.

  We would talk about everything.
  Some nights we would lose track
  and the morning sun would welcome us.

  We always made time for each other.

  But you don't have time
  for me anymore,
  only time for her.

I miss my friend.

There and Back Again

Mother,
when I was little, we used to play this game.

You had me squeeze my eyes shut
and take your hand
and we would go on a long walk,
swimming down city streets.

My clammy hands gripped your own tightly,
all my senses heightened –
swirling summer wind tickled my cheeks,
the smoldering scent of barbecue in the air,
and the chittering of birds,
their wings slapping the sky.

You steered us far away from our neighborhood
and then you had me open my eyes.
You revealed the world to me
and told me to lead you –
to find my way home.

You wanted to make sure, if I was ever lost,
I could find my way,
and somehow, I always knew the way back.

But maybe
never truly
the way forward.

Father,
you were a man
and I was a boy.

How was I to know
that it was the only way
we would ever know each other –
    from across the tracks –

    Always heading in the same direction
    but never on the same train?

I know it has been years now, but I'm so
sorry about your dad. I truly can't
imagine. ♡

Don't Let Go

For months and months now
I keep on having this dream
and it's so beautiful when I'm in it.

You're there with me
at your little house on Oak Street.
I can hear the TV on in the other room,
you're telling me jokes
and I can almost hear your deep
belly laugh.

Every time, it's a little bit different.

Sometimes you give me a hug
and I feel this great weight lifted,
sometimes we're eating dinner together,
and sometimes we're not there at all
and I have to find you,
but somehow, I always seem to know
where you are,
sometimes I find you in some new place,
like you've started a new life
somewhere far away.

But one thing is always the same:
no matter how many times
the dream keeps coming back to me,
when I wake up,
you're *still* gone.

Night Drive

On the nights I can't sleep
or I wake up thinking of you,
I go on one of those long drives
like we used to do.

I don't really know where I'm going,
sometimes it just feels good to drive,
    even if this is the only thing
        I have control over,
    at least I have something.

You used to be the one behind the wheel.
I was always too young,
    but I would navigate for you,
    and now I wish you could navigate
                for me.

You see,
I've been driving for hours and hours
and I've gotten myself lost
and I realize
    I can't trust myself to find the way.

I wish you were here
to tell me where to go
    when I've lost my way

      because I seem to be losing it
        more and more each day.

I've always struggled with
where I am in my life.

I live on the edge
of time,

One foot in the memories of the past,
one foot in the dreams of the future,

But stuck in the now —

The last place
I want to be.

I just don't want to be here —
anywhere but here.

I'm always here for you, even when "here" isn't
where you'd like to be. ♡

When did the days start to look like this?

    All I look forward to
        is the end of each day.

    But I don't want to go to sleep
        because then it will be tomorrow.

And tomorrow
    is just another today.

Moth Man

I met a girl today,
let's keep it simple and just call her A.

She was so radiant and warm,
I was drawn to her.

I was nervous at first,
too nervous to bring myself too close,
too afraid of being too forward,
too scared of being rejected.

But she smiled and she laughed at my jokes,
she took my hand and I felt confident
that she felt the same way I did.

The closer I drew to her,
the more her warmth engulfed me
and extinguished the chill in my bones.
And it was nice for a time.

She showed me what I could be
if I just got better,
so I strived to make her happy,
to make her proud

I learned to love the *idea* she had for me

I don't think you ever really loved me.

I think you loved the idea
of what I could be
for you.

How did it take me so long to see this?

Sometimes it's a gradual change when a relationship
morphs into something unhealthy and it's hard to see it
until you feel like youre in too deep.

Underneath

You enter the room
and I feel my breath **stop**.
I plunge down beneath the surface,
sinking – hiding in the depths from you.

I hold my breath
for as long as I can
and I hope it lasts the time
we are together.
I count down from ten
and wonder if I'll drown first
or if I'll get accustomed to the pain
and grow a set of gills.

I know
I can't come up for air, not yet,
because you'll see.

And as soon as you leave, I rush to the surface;
I exhale – I breathe in.

I've made it again

Lying in the darkness
with my cheek nestled into my pillow,
my eyes unburdened by any light,
I find my peace in this place.

Whispering wind through the window,
consoling my aching bones
and soothing my tired heart
from all the toils of the day.

The only voice here is the one within me,
winding down, slowly, to rest.

This stolen moment, out of time,
I hold tenderly in my soul,
and fall away from the somber, heavy head,
into the delights of wondrous dreams.

Writer's Therapy

I can't afford therapy,
so I guess I'll just have to write it all out.

Every morning, every night,
I open up and pour the problems on the pages.

But I still feel them hiding inside me,
clinging on for dear life,
tucked in the cracks,
tapping their feet at the back of my mind.

Why doesn't this work?
Why won't the pain go away?
Has it become a part of me?
The only things I write about anymore
are the things I want to forget.

Is my only worth as a writer
defined by the bad things
that have happened to me?

Why do I feel worse than when I started?
Why isn't this working?

Maybe this wasn't a good idea after all.

I think I better call it a day.

Your journals have been the only ones who truly listened to you for
so long, but they don't make for the best conversationalists.
I'm here for you if you ever want to talk.

There are so many paths to choose,
I find myself paralyzed with indecision.

I don't want to make the wrong choice.

If I could just find the door –
                    the one door

                to open

            to lead me into wherever
                my life is meant to go

        I could find peace.

I feel this so much. I think constantly searching for the right door
makes you stagnant and then complacent, and ultimately
even more unhappy . . . at least that's the case for me.

When we were young,
we wanted to be old.

When we became old,
we wanted to be young again.

But maybe
all we ever needed
was to be okay
with where we are.

I wish I was okay
with today.

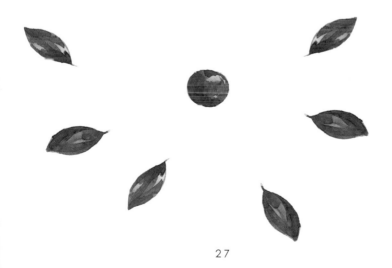

I am tired of the way things are –
   of the drifting through days
                      emptily.

I want to do something better,
   to be something better,
 than a hopeless soul
  in a hopeless vessel.

I want to break through the sky;
I want to swim with the stars;
I want to have dinner by candlelight
  with a girl with a smile behind her eyes;
I want to write a book
  and sell a copy to more than just
                one of my friends;
I want to be good enough.

I truly believe you will get there.
Because you are good enough.

The sky is heavy,
pushing down on us like a weighted blanket
with a force
greater than all the earth.

It is a comfort
to know how small we are,
to know we aren't responsible
for *everything*.

The pressure we feel
is nothing
compared to the height of the mountains,
the vastness of the skies,
the depths of the sea.

I feel like I can let go of it all
and everything will be okay.

This world has a way
of holding you tenderly.

Yes! I love this! I thought I was
the only one who thought this way!

Maybe Today (Part I)

Maybe today is the day
I start to do all the things I want to do.

Maybe I could try to be the person
I want to be.

Maybe.
Maybe I could start to live in the moment
rather than being stuck on the pain of yesterday
    or clinging to the hope of tomorrow –
        stringing me along with nothing to show.
Maybe I could get away
        from all these things dragging me down.

But
I'm so tired.
It's all getting so heavy.
I just wish I was ready to let go.

I just want to rest,
    is that too much to ask?

Maybe today,
I could lay down my head and get some sleep.

It's been so long
since I've had a good night's rest.

Some days
it is hard to be.

I get so anxious,
I feel paralyzed.

I cling too much to the familiar,
    even when I know it's wrong for me.

I'm afraid of not having
    the strength to move forward
            when it is time to.

        I feel like that time
            is coming

        and I'm so scared.

Do you ever just get tired?

Going through the motions
but not feeling any of them.

Doing whatever is required
but never what makes me happy.

It is exhausting.

I can only keep this up
for so long.

When will it break me?

Maybe tomorrow?
Maybe today?

It's not always going to be this hard, I promise.
And you don't have to go through this alone.

Therapy Session

I'm too much darkness
  and not enough daisies.
I try a smile out every day,
  but too often, it doesn't feel like me.
I am a marionette to my emotions
  and all I wish is that I could
  twist my neck around
  to better look at who is pulling the strings.
I'm tired of holding this heavy baggage,
  these streaming tears,
  these long and sleepless nights,
  these thoughts that don't make sense.
I want to be happy, I promise you,
I want to be.

When I was young,
alone, broken, and naïve,

I wished for myself some horrible tragedy
so that others might
notice, pity,
or even love me.

But when the tragedy I wished for
actually arrived,
I forgot all that,
and instead,
I felt all the pain
of the wish
I never should have made.

Burning Questions

When I saw the plumes of grey billowing up
    into the clouds, the policemen signaling
    my friend and I to turn around –
    the street off limits –
    what did I expect?

Who am I –
    that if any house should catch on fire,
    it should be mine?

What are the chances?
What memories were there that were so
   horrible they needed to be scorched away
                        from existence?

Where had the stories gone, the ones I'd
written, the ones that perished there,
    when all their pages had been burned?

Why did I cry like a wounded animal,
    writhing and twisting on the street,
    with judgmental strangers' eyes watching
    while my mother watched the house burn?

Why didn't they take him out?
    My dog – my father's puppy – my last link
    to everything I'd already lost?

How did he feel, my little friend,
    my sweet furry angel –
    when the smoke bit at his throat?
    Did he try to cry out like me?
    Did he wonder where I was
             when he couldn't breathe?

Too Many Bottles

Mom, look,
I know that in your head there's a lot of pain,
and you've got to find something to do
to keep from going insane.

But if it means
bringing down everyone with you,
then maybe it's just not the way.

You started with drinking
and maybe one is okay
even two or three every few days.

Maybe after number four,
you've already gone too far,
when you're screaming and crying
and you've consumed a whole bunch of pills
and run off out the door.

I can't get you to stop.

My sister's calling the cops,
but I still have to find you —
to hold you down until they get here
to pump your stomach,
to get out the pills
while you scramble and fight
and scream and bite
and I tell you I love you
but you push me away.

And it hurts so bad, but all I can say is,
"Everything is going to be okay."

Ragdoll

Do this – feel that –
House? Who needs it?
Dog? Who needs it?
Parents? Who needs them?
Childhood? Oh, grow up!
Money? You'll make it!
Dreams? Let's be real.
Love? You've got to settle sometime.

Rent? Where is it?
Job? Why don't you have it?
Ring? Why haven't you gotten it?
Question? Why haven't you asked it?
Kids? Why don't you want them?

You need to grow up.
You need to get help.
You need to commit.
You need to try harder.
You need to get over it.
You need to be realistic.

Run your fingers through my hair,
whisper in my ear,
remind me
that I am worth it

Oh friend, you've been through so much
So much hurt. So much trauma. You will heal in your
own time and in your own way, and I will be here in
whatever capacity you need.
You are more than the pain that consumes you. ♡

Who were we before,
sweet sister,
before we became this broken thing
that I cannot find a word for?

Do you remember our family,
when it was normal?
When you were simply my big sister,
and you didn't have to make all these sacrifices
to give me a better life?
Was I always this helpless?
Did you always have to pick me up,
to help me find the broken pieces of myself?

I think maybe I tried to hide the pieces
so you wouldn't find them,
in the hopes
that you would never know I was broken.

But I think you knew,
I think you always knew.

I'm sorry I didn't do a better job hiding it.

The Dream

I did it, I made it,
I'm out on my own two states away,
living with a bunch of strangers.

Sure, it's a little scary,
but I'm down in L.A.
This is good. It's good to be free.
I'm finally doing something,
something just for *me*.

There's nobody here to tell me what to do.
I still think about the things I left behind,
but mostly, *Dad*, I still think about you.

It's hard to get a job here.
I spent six months applying everywhere
within an hour of where I live.
Why do I still feel like a kid?
Why do I still need to ask my sister
for money?

Why is this so hard?

I left my old life behind, didn't I?
Why is it still finding me?
Why can't I sleep?
Why is it so hard to write?
Why do I still cry every night?

I think it was so brave of you to move there
and work toward your screenwriting dreams.
I'm sorry it was so hard though.

I still daydream about those California
   sun-kissed beaches:

   The gentle lapping of waves,
   the soft pulsing sounds they make,
   rhythmically lulling me into tranquility.

   They were my escape
   when my mind needed to ease,
   when my books were too great a labor.

   Where I could always go to find peace,
   where the sun and the world together
      cradled me gently
   and the problems and the drama
      were exhaled out
         onto the waves,
            to drift off and away . . .

This sounds so lovely

A and I moved down there together.

She and I weren't happy where we grew up —
we wanted more.

More from a world that taught us
good things are impossible
unless you're incredibly lucky.

We wanted to prove the world wrong,
to prove that a couple kids from nowhere
could be household names
if they were passionate enough.

We raised each other on hope,
fixed on tomorrow.

Our eyes drank the stars.
We shaped dreams from childhood scars,
and we talked about the future
like it could be anything
we wanted it to be.

Hope

I think it is brave
to hold hope close to you
when it seems so fragile and distant.

To stare the storm in the eye
and remain resolute,
grounded in your being,
unshaken in your willpower,
unstoppable.

So many things in this world
serve as constant reminders
of how powerless we are,
how futile our struggle is –
how unobtainable our dreams are –
how fleeting.

But still, I hope.

I'll Take the Check

I bought everyone a round of drinks
and I hear all their clinks
and I see all their smiles
and it's been a while
since I've felt this way,
but it makes me happy
that I just caused that feeling.

For the first time in a month,
I don't feel so pathetic.

Maybe it's all just empty,
but they're looking at me differently.
In their eyes, I don't see pity,
I don't see an outsider.

If I look close enough at them,
I see myself – *I see a liar.*

No, shut up, go away.

This is all I need, it's this moment.
I don't want to think
about the rent tomorrow
that I can't pay.

Here, I can be the hero
before I know my bank account
is less than zero.
Stay in this moment
because here, right now,
everything's okay.

I don't want to tell you
        the hurt

because you didn't cause it
        but you'll carry it like you did.

And it will hurt you
        like it's hurting me
                and that will just make it all worse.

So, I will hold this
        for a while
    until I can't
            anymore.

Push It Down

I'm sorry I'm not much in the mood to talk,
I've had a really hard day.

No, I hear you, you've had a hard day too.
No, go ahead,
I know you need to get it off your chest.
No, don't worry, this look wasn't meant for you.

I'm sorry, I didn't mean to make it worse,
you go ahead,
talk about whatever happened today.

I'm sorry you had a bad day.
No, I know, all you need is to feel close to me.
Here's a hug to make it better,
do you feel better?

You have so many questions for me,
I'll try to answer them all, okay?
I'll try to make you okay.
Can I make the bad day go away?
Can I give you my full attention?
Can I make you dinner?
Can I massage you?
Can I make it better?
Did I make it better?

You're sleeping peacefully beside me
and your arm is draped over my chest.

But I'm staring at the ceiling
and I think this is another night
where I won't get a wink of rest.

I can do this,
I've done it before
      so many times.

    Just pour your pain in me
    and let me carry it
    for the both of us.

I know what I'm doing.
I've got you.
I've been holding on to mine all this time
      and I've been able to hold it together.

    Just let me help you,

    Don't worry about me.

    I'll be okay,
      I promise . . .

Oh my friend . . . I think you know this isn't a
sustainable solution forever.

Pedestal

When we met,
you said I was perfect
and who doesn't want to be perfect?

You put me up on some pedestal
and I used to think it was sweet,
but I didn't know then
that it was made of glass.

I am afraid to move —
to crack this beautiful thing
and topple down to the earth.

You seem to think I'm something more
than I could ever be —
something I never was to begin with.

That's a lot of pressure
to put on someone
and I don't know how much longer
I can keep it up.

I'm sorry,
but I can't measure up
to the me
you have in your head.

Something must be wrong with me
because she is perfect,
but it still doesn't feel right.
     Why doesn't it feel right?

My hands are overflowing
     with gold dust,
          but it's slipping through my fingers –
               blowing away.

               Why don't I chase it?
               Why don't I want to?

Today, I love her.

But what if tomorrow I don't?

Love shouldn't feel like this,
               should it?

No . . . it shouldn't

I'm Trying to End Things

I think we should break up.
I'm sorry it's hard to hear,
but it's hard to say.

You're overbearing.
I feel like I can't be myself with you.

You call me up every night
when you're heading to sleep
and it's always when I sit down to write.
You want me to talk to you,
but you always have nothing to say.

And I can't tell you what I want to say –
that I'm not okay, that I'm never okay.

No, you're right, I guess, we can work on this,
we don't have to break up
if that's what you really want.

I know you're happy with me.
I'm sorry I'm not happy.
I wish I *was* happy.

I feel like I'm eating for two,
I don't know what else to do.

But I really think I need a break from you.

This must be so exhausting for you. When you sacrifice your
happiness, it starts to make you feel like you never deserved it in
the first place.

I am strong.
I am strong.
I am strong, yes, of course.

I will be strong enough for you.
I will be strong enough for two.
I will find a way.
I can do it.
I can.
I have to do this –

                for you.

      I can do this.
      I know you need me to.

            I will . . .
            I have to . . .
            I can . . . I can . . . I . . .

                I can't . . .

Holding Hands with a Ghost

When I was ready to let go,
I realized what it was you were really
holding on to.

You cling to all of these parts of me,
but I'm not made of those parts
anymore.

I have long outgrown that person you hold.
You cling to the dust
you imagine me to be,
but I have moved on
and maybe
you should too.

53

WINTER

Bitter

All the old and tired weathered away,
raw and stripped down to nothing,
exposed bare bones,
battered by the elements.
Endurance tested by hard snows
and long, frigid, dark winter nights.

Stark and harsh and bleak and unforgiving.
These days, the only warmth is what is left
within – what small flame flickers to soothe a
chill down to the marrow,
ready to be extinguished with a wink.

I am bare and hollowed out
and the heavy whiteness blankets everything
all around me.

These days are the shortest of the year,
and the hardest to trudge through
with darkness looming around each corner.

It seems so strange to me,
I was born on the first day of winter,
yet it is the season in which
I've never felt like I am meant to exist.

Hibernate

I am cold.

I think I have been freezing for years,
buried beneath the dirt,
only a couple feet down in the earth.

Nobody knows I'm here.

Maybe I like it this way,
I don't know – I don't remember
what life was like at the surface.

But I feel myself slowly waking up
and I'm nervous to see
what I will find up there.

"I'm still here!"
    I scream out at the world.

"I still matter.
 I still feel pain and anger and hatred,
 even when I hold it in
 or don't express it
 because I can't find the words
 or I'm too afraid to say them.

I still hurt
 and long for love.
 I'm still here, breathing.

Do not forget about me
 because I have not forgotten you."

        And no one responds.

"Hi!" I respond, "I haven't forgotten you!
And I'm always here for you, and I'll always listen."

I have heard
there is a giant within me,
something far greater than I.

There are days
when he shakes the walls,
when he wants to be heard.

He wonders when I'll find him,
and I wonder where he's hiding.

♡

I'll hold it together,
even though I know
we're falling apart,
because I know it's what you need.

I'll do this for you
even though I don't want to.

I can't remember the last
whole day I spent happy.

But every day,
I see you smiling obliviously.

Maybe this is how it's supposed to be.

Everything I do
seems to be for you.

I forget what it is that I want.

I get so tangled up in you,
I can't pull myself free.

I can't seem to remember
where your desires end
and where my own begin.

Every single piece of you
has become a part of me.

I've nearly forgotten
what I look like
without you.

Maybe, when you feel ready, taking some time to
do some self-discovery — getting reacquainted with
yourself and the things that bring you joy might be a
nice thing to do! ♡

Every morning,
I stare at myself in the mirror
             and practice my smile.

I think of all the references:
smiling friends, laughing at jokes,
spellbound lovers grinning,
kindness on strangers' faces.

I wonder what it feels like
to be that happy.

I practice smile after smile
  and try to convince myself
             I look happy.

        But I never do,
     I always see through it.

And now, I'm starting to get worried
          everyone else does too.

I had a good day today
and I should be happy;
I should be grateful for the good days.

Something must be wrong with me
because I have no reason
to be unhappy

and yet,
I still find a way.

What's wrong with me?

Nothing is.

The Smoking Man

"I'll be okay, I'll have just one more,"
Dad always said, grinning
before he lit up another.

"Don't ever start doing this yourself.
It'll kill you, you know,"
he would say, but I don't think he knew.

His heart stopped
    sometime between dusk and dawn,
as he sunk back in his favorite recliner,
blackened ashtray at his right,
his head tilted back, mouth slouched open,
pallid cheeks once gleaming,
his body swallowed up by too much cushion
and too much tired,
welcomed in by endless sleep.

I wonder if he had regrets
sitting there, at the eleventh hour.

I wonder how tired one has to get
to fall asleep and never wake back up again.

Just one cigarette too many
was all it took to stop a man
    old as oak roots sunken deep in the earth,
    bones strong and resilient as tree trunks,
    heart young and singing of summer,
but falling silent to make way for winter's kiss.

Dad,
I have not forgotten you.

Someday soon,
the number of days we've spent apart
will exceed
the number of days we spent together.

But those were good days,
and though you aren't with me anymore,
you are still here.

Wherever I go,
I take you with me.

♡♡

I've been asked,
"What were the last words he said to you?"

To be honest, I don't know.
I don't remember.
It's not that I've forgotten them
                but that I never knew.

When he died,
it had been a week since I'd seen him.

Do you remember the last thing you said
                to someone a week ago?

Slowly I'm losing his voice from my brain.

        I don't have any voicemails saved.
        I don't have any of his home videos.
        All I have are memories and pictures
            I'm holding on to tightly,
            but I know
            that once the last memory fades away,
                my dad will be gone forever.

I'm so sorry. I've loved hearing the stories you've told me
about him; he sounds like he was quite a character!

Lying Awake in the Dark

I can't sleep.

I'm restless;
my mind turning over thoughts like pages,
cold unraveled sheets spread across my bed,
while I'm looking up at the ceiling,
up at the night sky beyond it.

I can see them,
stars like freckles dotting your shoulders.

Distant bright lights, companions
to hold my hands tight on either side,
telling me it's going to be alright, saying,
All you have to do
is play the long game.

It will be a long night
if you stay up too late.

It's too early in the morning
to feel too alright.

Just say goodnight
or you'll be uptight all night,

Wishing for better days
that aren't ready to come, son.

Goodnight stars,
night night.

"It's Not That Hard"

I know
it's easier to be happy
if I just force myself to smile,

                    but I can't.

I know
the way I feel is a mindset
that I just have to change,

                    but I can't.

I know
I need to stop tearing myself down,

                    but I can't.

I know
I just keep finding excuses to stay in bed
when there might be
so much waiting for me outside
if I could just get up,

                    but I can't.

Grief (Part 1)

It always happens
when everything is fine,
when it has no reason to be here with me,
when I have let my guard down
and foolishly believed
it had left for good
and I would be able to forget it.

Maybe a look
or a word
or even just a thought,

And the pouring comes down,
it soaks every corner of my body,
every corner of my heart.

I cannot escape the flash flood
washing over me,
forcing me down,
even as I struggle
and fight for breath.

I am *nothing*
compared to the power it has over me.

You're more powerful than you give yourself credit for.
You haven't let the grief consume you. ♡

Don't all fathers pass things on
        to their children?

    They watch them grow up,
      they struggle to tell them
                how proud they are,
    and they fear their children
                making their own mistakes.

Maybe the thing I'm most scared of
        in becoming a father
        is a child ending up like me.

I think a child who ended up like you would be
lovely.

The Hardest Day

I remember where my mind was,
back in seventh grade
on the hardest day of my life.

When I looked at myself and wondered
what the world would be like
if I wasn't in it.

Would they finally be happy,
the ones who didn't want me around?

I looked at myself in the mirror
and thought I finally understood
all the things they said about me.

All day, I wrote little notes to myself;
how I could do it,
who would find me.

I crumpled some of them up
and threw them away.

I don't know who found them,
but I was taken to the office.
They called my parents.
I still remember their faces.
I was watching because I wondered
if they really cared.

I saw so much hurt and pain and confusion
and I promised myself
I would never think that way again.

I'm so glad you decided that.

Misconceptions

You think
because I exude confidence
that I am cocky,
    but you don't know
    I try to be confident
    to hide the doubt.

You think
because I am kind
that I am flirty,
    but you don't know
    I'm trying every day
    to brighten a world
    that only ever wants to be dark.

You think
because I seem normal
that my life is easy,
    but you don't know
    the pain I have endured,
    the scars I cover up,
    or the words I bottle up inside.

You think
you have me all figured out,

but you never asked me
my name.

Prisoner

I hear the footsteps pacing
back and forth.

I try to speak,
but it tells me to shut up.

I try to exhale,
but it tells me to hold my breath.

I try to tell myself
that I'm okay,
but I'm not,
I'm just the prisoner
in my own head

and I'll *never* let myself forget.

I look in the mirror
and I see someone weak,
             so weak.

Anger boils up inside me.
All I can think is,

"I hate you.
 I wish I didn't have to
 share this body with you.
      You make me sick.
      I wish I could throw you up
        and leave you behind –
                 forgotten."

Oh friend. I wish you saw yourself the way I see you.
I think you're more amazing than I could ever put into
words.

Hands shaking,
back and forth,
to an uncertain rhythm,
sometimes fast
or maybe slow,
moved by unseen strings;
grief, fear, anxiety –
the playful puppeteers.

Their voices ring,
Nothing,
you are nothing

Hitting – **beating**
against my head,
shaking no more, no –
a **fist** instead.

It beats me,
it beats me red.

Release. Silence.
Steady hands.

Control
is mine again.

Maybe Today (Part II)

Maybe today is the day
  I end it all.
If it's the only way I can feel okay.

I could finally rest.

I would be back with my dad.
He could hold me close.
I miss his arms around me,
they made me feel so safe.

What would I ask him? What would I tell him?
  Were you proud of me, Dad?
  Was I good enough for you?
  Did you see me walk at graduation?
    Were you walking beside me?
  I wish you would've told me you knew.
  I wish I could've said goodbye.
  I wish you could've taught me
   so many things,
    like how to drive
    or how to be okay
   because there's so much
    I still don't know.

He would probably tell me
he's disappointed in me
for coming to see him
sooner than I was supposed to.

It feels like the only way
    to get away from the pain.
It feels like the easy way out,
    but my life has never been easy.
Living sounds so much harder.
I just want to run away.
    I'm so scared I won't make it,
    I'm so scared of making mistakes.

It hurts and I can't help but fall down.
I'm getting too used to living my life
    facedown on the ground.
I'm a mess and I don't know if I'll be okay,
    but maybe it's better to feel this way
    than to feel nothing at all.

Maybe today
    isn't the day.

Hey now, you wrote another poem where you said you
wouldn't think of doing this again. I'm holding you to that —
I don't want to lose you. And you're not ready to see your
dad again yet. You have more life to experience for him, and
for yourself. ♡

I waited and waited
    and the seasons turned
    and the buildings crumbled
    and the memories faded
    and my body wore away
               with age
    and the dead flesh
        peeled from my cold bones
    and there was nothing left.

And you decided then
        that you were ready
               to love me.

I care too much
about things,
about people
who don't care enough
about me.

I see it happening every day
only I can't stop myself –
they need me.

Maybe one day
they'll see it.

We need to get some more positive people in your
life! Come out with everyone after work on Friday,
okay? It'll be fun, I promise.
(And we can leave whenever you want to)

Glass Always Empty

You were feeling low
  and you found comfort in me,
    so you took it for yourself.

You drank the happiness
  from my bones
  and you felt new.

Maybe, to be fair, you didn't know
just how low I was feeling too.

Now I'm empty,
  I'm struggling to stay on my feet,
    and I'm feeling worse than I did before.

But I see you're smiling
and you want another glass,
so I promise
      I won't say a thing.

You don't have to love others at the expense of yourself.
♡

There's a voice in the back of my head,
and it's your voice,
but I'm tired of listening to it.

I'll tell you right now:
I am enough
and I always have been.

If you cannot see that,
it is not my fault
or up to me
to make you see.

Yesss!! ♡♡♡

Doormat

Too long have I done
    what others wish of me,
too long have I stepped aside
    or let others step over me,
too long have I been unhappy.

Too long have I wanted
    to say goodbye to you.

        I'm starting to fear
           that when the right moment comes,
          I won't find the courage.

I think you'll surprise yourself — you have more
courage than you see in yourself. ♡

Sometimes,
I think that I am doomed.

Because what if
I leave her
and no one else
will ever love me again?

Why would they,
when I can't even love myself?

"What are those bumps on your face?"

"Do they hurt?"

"I hope I don't get those when I grow up."

"I can't even look at you,
you're disgusting.
Those bumps are so gross."

       – Dealing with acne at sixteen
      while being torn apart
            by a five-year-old girl
            while I'm at work,
            surrounded by staring people,
            too embarrassed to say
                anything at all

This makes me so angry on your behalf; I wish I could have been there to help. She never realized how deep her words cut into you.

There's no place
for me to go
when I want to escape myself.

I wish I could crawl
out of my own skin.

I'm trying to think about myself
for once.

Selfishly,
I hope that
long after we've grown apart,
you remember me.

I don't want to be forgettable.

I didn't know
what to do,

so I ended things with you

and I saw you hurt,
and I saw you cry.
and I know that I caused all that
and I'm so sorry.

I hated myself
and I still do.

Maybe it would be easier for you
if you hated me too.

A Poem about a Breakup

She came over for the weekend,
but I knew it was only going to be for a day.

I worked up the courage to tell her
that I had something difficult to say.

It was the hardest thing I've ever had to do,
but it felt right
because *we* didn't feel right anymore.

And I owed her that,
I owed myself that.

We sat down on the bed in my room
and I laid everything out;
my reasons,
my feelings,
that I wasn't going to change my mind.

She didn't understand,
she thought everything was alright,
she thought we would be together *forever*,
she thought I was being impulsive,
she thought she knew who I was,
                    who we were.

She cried and she cried
but I made sure not to hold her,
as hard as it was –
I thought that would only confuse her.

She shook and she wept
and she watched me.

She told me I'm changing,
I need therapy,
I have issues and I need to figure them out.
I knew she was right to some extent,
but that didn't change my decision.

She left that day;
she walked out the door
and out of my life.

I've never made someone cry more
than she did that day.

How do you deal with the guilt?

The hardest things to do in life often require having the courage to make a change, even when it is heart-wrenching to do so. But life always balances itself out – with great pain comes great joy. That applies to both of you, and maybe now you'll both have the room to grow into happier people.

What I told you
  was tender,
  was secret.

What I told you
  was sacred,
  was difficult to share.

But it was for you
  because I could trust you
      and I knew I could let you in.

But you told them,
  you told everyone
  and you diminished it
  and you diminished me.

      You made me small
      and insignificant
      and you made
        what I gave to you –
        what was once special –
              meaningless.

It's unfortunate all that happened.
I really hope things can be resolved between you
guys, but that's a hard hurt to heal I know.

You take me back
to fourth grade,
when they surrounded me
and punched me in the stomach
again and again and again
until I couldn't breathe.

Thank you
for reminding me
to be careful
who I can trust.

Everyone seems to think
  loneliness is a sad thing.

But it can be a comfort too.

At least I know
  I always have myself,
  even when it seems
  everyone else has left.

I've always been afraid
of losing people close to me.

It feels inevitable
and sometimes,
maybe in anticipation,
I drive them away

before they have the chance
to leave me themselves.

Pitiful admirable

Weak strong

Stupid smart

Powerless powerful

Insignificant important

Small tall

Nothing everything

Feeble talented

Helpless inspiring

Naïve trusting

Unable capable

Inadequate amazing

Pathetic honorable

Insufficient worthy

Puny noticeable

Little brave

Not in control not responsible for everything

Not enough enough

Never enough always enough

Head spinning, dizzy,
choking on absent breath.

Can't stop crying.

I taste the stomach bile,
vomit, retch.

Shaking fingers,
shaking fist,
striking myself – my head.

Maybe if I bleed.

No, better to be empty,
hollow,
and dead.

You may think you hate me.

But I can promise you,
nobody hates me more than myself.

Cocoon

I feel safe in the ground
where there's no one around.

No voices to have to listen to,
no expectations
or comparisons to live up to.

Just me and the dirt
huddled all around me,
the darkness snuggling in close.

Six feet down,
no one can hurt me,
no one can be disappointed.
No one knows
where I am.

I'm safe in my cocoon.

Confessions (or I'll Never Forget)

In kindergarten, my parents got divorced
   because I couldn't save their marriage.

In first grade,
I thought I was the smartest kid in the class.

In second grade,
I was the weird kid everyone avoided.

I peed my pants in class in third.

I switched schools in fourth grade
  and was jumped on my way home from school.
I pushed down a little kid
  and broke his front teeth.

I got suspended in fifth grade.

I switched schools again in sixth.

In seventh grade, I almost killed myself.

In eighth grade, I made fun of a girl
  who asked me to a dance
  because I thought she was going to
         make fun of me.

First day of freshman year,
I found out my dad died.
    I didn't cry for two weeks.
That year, I broke up with a girl
    before she could break up with me.
    She cut herself,
    but I never got back with her.

The summer after my sophomore year,
my house burned down with my dog inside.
      All I could do was watch –
      why was that all I could do?

Junior year, I lied to some who gave me money.

My senior year, I lied to my mom
   and moved out when she was at her lowest,
   drowning at the bottom of a bottle –
I left her there to drown, while she went to jail.

I moved down to L.A.
I thought I was better than everyone around me
and I forgot my sister's birthday
               three years in a row.

I couldn't get a job out of school.
I worked dead-end jobs and gave up my dreams.

I dated a girl who thought I was the one
and never had the courage to break up with her.
We fought and took a break
      and I saw another girl.
She never knew, when we got back together.
She moved back home with me.

I lost one of my best friends that year
      all because of a misunderstanding
      and he meant more to me than he knew.

I broke up with her.
I'm still picking up the pieces.

I am the greatest at messing up
      the most beautiful things.

I don't deserve
    to be your friend.

You held me up
    when I couldn't walk,
you took me in
    when the sprinkles began to pour,
and you held me in your arms
    when I cried,
    when I deserved
        to be alone.

I know you — and you make yourself sound so much worse
than you really are. But you're worth every good day, and
every bad day too. You're one of my best friends, and I'm
never going to walk away from you.

I wish I could have you tell me,
"I love you"

louder than I can tell myself,
"I hate you,"

but my voice just keeps
drowning yours out.

Sometimes,
   I turn against myself

   and the only one
   fighting for me

      is **you**.

Put 'em up!!

Thank you
for being there for me
when I couldn't be

for myself.

For holding on to me
when I tried so hard
to push you away.

For loving me when
all I could see
were the worst parts of myself.

SPRING

Awakening

Starting soft mornings with sweet songs
to welcome weather-worn ears.
The colorful displays are filling in
and hope, long dormant, tucked in the depths,
protrudes up from the cracks,
realizing its moment has come
and now, reinvigorated.

A tender, young, vibrant hopefulness,
maybe somewhat small and fragile now,
but compacted with so many possibilities,
expanding and spilling with light and growth.
Leaves reaching toward the sun,
asking for aid with humility
and a youthful eagerness.

These days are a gentle blossoming,
an unfolding of beauty, an uncovering,
a revealing of what is beneath –
what has been budding and forming,
waiting for the opportune moment to become.

These are the days to focus on the valleys
ahead, the earth awakening anew.

These are the days for healing.

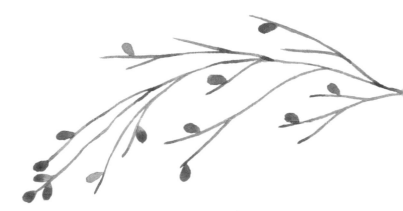

When I let go of her,
I felt all the air rush back
into my lungs.

The air
she told me
it was not okay to breathe.

"I am alone!"

    I screamed out
at the stars,
expecting silence.

    But what I heard instead
was my own beating heart.

You were wandering through the world
and you cut your foot
on some part of me.

And though you were bleeding,
you found all the other
pieces of me,
scattered apart,

and you found the way
they went back together

until I was whole again.

Someday,
I'll look at these scars
and see the strength
beneath them.

But maybe
not today.

And that's okay.

I'm tired of being afraid
of making a mistake
that I will always regret.

I'm tired of being afraid
of losing everything I have
when there is so much I could gain.

I'm tired of being afraid
of who I might become
if I stop bottling my emotions.

I'm tired of being held back
from making any choices.

I am tired of letting the fear
of what might happen
take hold of me.

I will try to learn
to live with the fear,
to make choices
and know that it's okay
if I make a mistake.

♡ ♡ ♡

Hey Dad

It's been a while since we've talked,
   but it's because I haven't known what to say.
Some days you make me so angry
   and some days you make me okay.

I hate the way your memories
are carved on my heart.
It's been ten years and I still remember
your voice, your face, the way you looked at me,
      the way you were proud,
         even when I was ashamed or embarrassed.

I hate that I still think about you,
   that despite all this time,
      these wounds haven't even healed.

I hate that I miss you,
   that I still dream about you,
   and when I wake up, I still cry
      because you're still gone.

I hate that you taught me
   to try and try and try again and never give up
   because I've been trying
      and I'm tired and my eyes are red
      but you won't let me go to bed —
      I can't get your words out of my head.

I hate that you can't be here,
   that it has to be enough
   to remember your arms around me.

I hate that nobody else understands,
   and they say they do,
   but how could they know this pain
     when they didn't have these thoughts,
     these feelings – when they didn't have you?

I hate that you'll never meet her.
   She's so perfect and you left before
              she even came.
I hate that I'm crying
   and I know this grief will go away
   and come back when I least expect it,
     but you won't.

I hate that you're hearing every word
   and you're smiling and you're proud,
   because it's not enough for me.

I hate that I can't bring you back,
   not with a book – not with a poem.

I hate that this poem is the closest I'll ever get
   to another one of your hugs.

I hate that as much as I want to,
            I *can't* hate you.

       And I can't let you go.

Thank You, Sister, for Being My Mother

I knew Mom was hurting.
I wanted to help.
I knew I could be there
    when she was ready to heal.

I know you just wanted to protect me.

I know bad things happen to good people,
even though it isn't fair.

But I had to be there for her
when her world was on fire.
You knew
    I couldn't pick up the pieces for her.
You knew
    because you already tried.

But I wouldn't listen to you,
    telling me to get away from her,
because I just had to stay –
to be there for her
when she was ready to ask for help.

And she broke my heart
and you knew it was coming,
    but I wouldn't believe you.

    You didn't say, "I told you so."
    You just held me tight
        and took me in
            when I cried.

Self-Reminder #1

If you try to feel everyone else's pain,
eventually it will be too much to handle.

And then you won't even
be able to handle
your own.

Sometimes it's really hard being so empathetic —
having these emotional boundaries helps so much in
making happiness sustainable.

Elephants

How do we start over, Mom?
Do we try to go back to before?
Or do we find a new way forward?

Do we have to be different people now,
or do we just be ourselves?

You tell me stories
from A.A., from prison, from church,
and I'm learning this new person
                              you're becoming.

There are all these elephants in the room –
a whole herd, in fact, and
I don't know what I can ask, what I can say.
I don't really know what to do,
    or what I want to know about the new *you*.

I'm sure there were days
you felt so small, so powerless beneath it all,
and other days,
you felt like you couldn't help
knocking things over.

I know some of those feelings –
the guilt, the shame, the self-hate,
the vulnerability in everyone knowing.

And I know another thing, you and I –
we're both still learning how to love ourselves

I love that despite everything, you are still so capable of
empathy.

116

She's been sober now
for almost a year.

And every day
the weight of that grows bigger
and bigger
and bigger.

I only hope
one day
she doesn't crumble beneath it.

I used to think
if I waited patiently long enough,
things would change
all on their own.

One day I realized —

I can change them *now*.

I Don't Hate You,
but I Still Have to Say Goodbye

Maybe my words weren't enough
or these hands simply didn't embrace you well

Maybe we were never going to last
as long as we wished we would
and we spent all our time trying to catch rain
slipping through our fingers

Maybe what was wrong
wasn't me and wasn't you

Maybe it was *us* who never belonged,
or maybe we did – but only for a time

Maybe it's okay to grow apart and change
and find someone else to grow old with –
to not linger on the things that were
and instead start to look forward to
new things that are coming –
the new people,
the new *I love you*'s,
the new hands and lips and memories

Maybe it's okay if we find it in ourselves
to move on and find a new way to be

Everything will work itself out some way;
maybe we will be okay.

Letting someone go emotionally is always a much
longer and much harder type of goodbye. ♡

"It's what I'm used to"
 isn't a good reason to stay

and

"This is harder than I thought it would be"
 isn't a good reason to leave.

Yes!! ♡

Moving On

When you picked me up
off the shelf,
I was *new.*

You breathed me in,
filling your nose with
my fresh book smell.

And for a while I was your *favorite* book.
You took me with you wherever you went.
You read my pages over and over
and handled me gingerly, tenderly.

But then, one day,
you put me back on the shelf,
and I began to gather dust.
You always knew
I would be there, waiting,
if you needed me.

Only when you came back
to find me, years down the road,
did you discover I was gone,
picked up and stolen away
by someone
who still saw
the magic
in my pages.

I know it sounds dramatic,
but I used to think
it would be easier to die
than to break up with her
and cause her that much pain.

It gets easier though,
if you let it,
if you can forgive yourself.

Sometimes
we have to break a heart along the way
                            to mend our own.

I'm still mending every day,
and I'm happy
I chose to keep living,
even when that felt like
the more difficult choice.

Because it was always the right one.

This is so important — self forgiveness is so so so
hard, but so important I'm really glad you're on that
path.

Self-Reminder #2

I don't know how many times
I stopped myself
from doing something
I needed to do

because of someone else
who wanted something different
from me.

Your needs matter, too;
you have worth
and it's okay
to make a choice someone doesn't agree with.

Their happiness cannot come
at the cost of your own.

♡ ♡

Second Chances

If one day you look in the mirror
and you no longer recognize yourself,

If you've been wearing a mask too long
and you've forgotten what's underneath,

Please,
be brave enough
to shed the skin
   you've found yourself walking around in,

Be brave enough
to find yourself –
to discover who you really are.

You might not like everything you find,
but that's okay –
this is not the end.

Be brave enough
to change who you are –
to try your best,
to be someone you can be proud of.

       And be gentle with yourself,
          be tender and patient
          and loving and kind.

       These things take time.

I'm so proud of you for doing all this. I know growth isn't linear,
but you are doing so well. I love seeing you smile more!

An Ode to Debbie

There's a voice that speaks before I do.
It lives down in the back of my brain
and it's made a cozy little nest there.

Whenever it hears something kind about me
from my lips or someone else's,
it doesn't hesitate to speak up.

It is my grumpy neighbor on the bottom floor
who hits the ceiling with a broom
whenever I get too loud, too excited, too happy.

It likes to play whack-a-mole
with any compliments
that show up uninvited.

An overactive self-defense mechanism
designed to shut out
and shut down anyone it doesn't trust
that has long forgotten the difference
between the words *friend* and *enemy.*

I feed it honesty and it likes that.
It's slowly learning to trust me.
Someday, maybe I'll get close enough
to shut it down.

I'm still learning how to stop the self-hate,
but most days it's automatic.

When I am weak,
please
gather me up in your arms
and take me to places
I don't have the strength to see.

I've gotchu ♡

Maybe Today (Part III)

Maybe today is the day
I start to get better.

I'm not there yet,
but I'm starting to see
just what that life could be.

I'm starting to realize
getting better isn't going to just
happen overnight.

It'll take a lot of work along the way.
It'll be a long time before I feel alright
and it sucks, but you know what?

Maybe that's okay
if I can learn how to feel
just a little bit better every day.

I didn't used to be like this.
I had dreams once,
maybe I can have them again.

If I could just get out of this funk I'm in,
maybe I could be something,
maybe I could do something that I'm proud of

Maybe tomorrow holds more for me
than today.

My sweet sister,

whose love gave me hope,
whose sunshine parted rainstorms,

so sweet and so wholesome.

I'm afraid
I can't be all that you want me to be.

Your little brother
has to become a man.
I've been through so much,
but you have to *let go* to let me grow.

Self-Reminder #3

It's okay to not be so hard on yourself,
to wear your pain on your face.

Give yourself a little time to let go,
to fall down and crumble
and get back up when you're ready.

It's okay to let yourself feel,
even if it's painful.

When my knuckles grow white,
when my eyes glisten,
when my cheeks fill in red,
when my jaw clenches,
when my mouth hangs open,
when I'm so filled with anger or despair
  that I've forgotten who I am . . .

> Will you take my hand?
> Will you call my name
>   and bring me back?
> Will you remind me
>   who I am
>   when I forget?

Deal. Will you help me when I feel this way too?

Take a moment,
close your eyes,
and listen to the sea –
the soothing lull of the waves.

Sink down
beneath the surface.
Deeper,
deeper,
deeper still,
until you can't hear the wind,

you can't see the light,

and you can't smell

the salt in the air.

Sink inside yourself
and find the peace
within.

I love this imagery — so soothing. ♡

Armor

When you're always the outcast
 and you're used to being prodded at,
when every joke is at your expense –
 then every smile makes you suspicious;
when they always tell you who you are
 and never ask you,
when you get pushed around too long
 and you have to learn
 to stand up for yourself
 because it seems like no one else will,
when you're used to *everyone*
 being an enemy,
it can be hard to turn that off.
It can be hard to not snap
 at the wrong people –

 the people who love you.

 I'm sorry for that.

These brittle bones
break
under the weight of a whisper,

but rebuild
to move **mountains**.

♡ ♡

Sister, I hope you're proud of me.

I wrote a book of poetry.
I'm currently writing number two.

I know it's not the stuff you like,
and it gets a little dark at times.
I don't mind if people see
this vulnerable side of me,
but I hope it's good enough for you.

I always wanted to make you proud.
You were always there for me.

Thank you for everything you did.

I wouldn't be where I am right now,
if you hadn't made so many sacrifices.

I know we are different people now,
but that doesn't mean we'll grow apart.
I still love you, I hope you know.

Sister, I hope you're proud of me.

I know she is

I am learning how to do things for myself.
I go to bed at a decent time.
I try really hard to speak up
for myself.

I'm learning how to say no
and how to walk away
if I don't feel okay.

I try to remember
it's okay to let myself be vulnerable.

I write down how I feel every day.

I'm still working on me.
I catch myself talking me down.
I stop playing the "what if" games.
I let myself cry —
but not for the whole night.

I am making progress.

No matter how many times
I've torn myself down,
you keep building me up,
and in doing so,
you've taught me how
        to build myself up.

    You believe so much in me
    I'm starting to believe too.

And you're doing amazing — your hands don't shake
from anxiety nearly as much as they used to, have
you noticed that?

I got caught up in
all the things
I wanted to do,
I wanted to be.

I forgot that I am **here**
and that is good too.

I find the darkness follows me.
It is always there, lingering,
waiting for me to turn back,
to acknowledge it.

I know it is there,
         taking me in, in all its forms,
         but as long as I don't turn,

         it will always be at my back
         and nothing more.

I'm Working on Things

I still try to avoid mirrors
because they remind me too much
of all the things I don't like about myself.
I still don't eat healthy enough
or work out enough.
I still run out of breath before my legs run out.
I still get anxiety around mannequins.
I still wonder how I managed to convince
tens of thousands of people
to read my words.

But I smile now more days than I cry
and when it rains,
I don't lock myself in the dark anymore.
Instead, I use it as an excuse
to cuddle up in a blanket and read a good book.

I try to start off every morning
with a compliment for myself.
Something nice like,
Your clothes match or maybe even *You're not bad.*

Okay, I'll admit, I'm still working on it.

I still have bad days,
but I'm starting to get better.

Life has so many seasons,
  it's never too late to change.

You can always pack up and move
    somewhere new;
you can always stop
    something you don't like about yourself;
you can always ask questions –
    even if you don't get answers;
you can always say no;
you can always pick up a new hobby
    and maybe you won't be good at it
                        for a while
              but you'll get better;
you can always laugh at yourself.

You can always pick up the pieces
                    and start over.

You can always change.

I found myself
  in all the places I hated,

so I became
      someone *else*.

I love this — you can work all you want on trying to
be better but that can only go so far if you stay in
environments or around people that hinder your growth!

I want to
love myself
the way
you love me,

Only,
I don't know how
to overlook all the things
I hate about myself.

Please Don't Lie to Me

Don't tell me
I'm wonderful
when I know how terrible I am.

Don't tell me
I'm sweet
when I know I do the cruelest things.

Don't tell me
I'm handsome
when I know I'm ugly.

Don't tell me
I'm worth it
when I know I'm not.

You're the only one
who tells me these things.

So, they can't
possibly
be true.

I don't lie to you. So, they are most definitely true.

I forgive you.

For all the *years* of cruel words,
   all the times you tore me down,
     or tripped me at the start
         of the race.

For all the times you doubted me –
   told me I was incapable;
       worthless, not worthy.

For making me believe
   my voice didn't matter.
For being my harshest critic
   and the first person to
     ruin my good days with rain.

I forgive you for everything.

Let's start over.

> *– The words I should've
> said to myself sooner*

YASSSS!!! ♡ ♡ ♡

Sitting here, wasting the day away,
with nothing to watch but the clock hands,
turning my mind in circles.

Sometimes I think all my friends
have outgrown me.

They don't really call anymore.
They don't show up at my door.

Getting older, I sort of get it,
there's only so many minutes in a day,
there's only so many words you can say.

Time steals everyone away from us,
but it's not our fault.
Sometimes people just change,
they aren't avoiding us.

I need to learn
to stop blaming myself for everything,
to let go of the things beyond my control:
the seasons,
the inevitability of change,
and the loss of friends.

Losing friends is so hard. Making new ones is hard too.
But I'm really grateful that I have you.

Lost Friend

I hope you remember me
long after we no longer speak.
I hope I cross your mind
when you drive past the streets we walked.

I hope you smile to yourself
when something reminds you
of a memory we shared
or a joke I told you.

I hope it all meant something to you
                        like it did to me.

I hope you are happy,
wherever your life has taken you.

I hope you think about calling me too.

Self-Reminder #4

You take on so many things
for other people
and you don't think twice
because that's just
who you are.

But don't forget,
it's okay to be
a little selfish
every now and then.

Maybe *selfish* is the wrong word.

I used to think
there was some aspect of me
that drove people away
      when you lose a parent,
      when you lose a mentor
        who moves far away from you
        and never writes,
      when you lose a friend
        over something so trivial,
      when you lose a pet
        whose life can never be long enough.

I started to leave things
  before they could leave me.

  Or never let myself get close enough
      to be sad
      when they inevitably left.

But I couldn't help myself with you,
    I couldn't help but fall in love.

    I am changed, it seems, because
      I've never been more afraid
        than I am now
        of losing you.

You won't lose me, I promise.
You matter more to me than you realize . . .

When were these moments, I wonder,
when we became separate people
from the children we grew from –
these moments we unknowingly became
who we are now –
how did we miss this?

Make Myself Proud

I miss the naïve little boy in me
who believed he could change the world.
　When did he grow up?
He used to believe I could be anything.
　Can I go back to being his hero?

When did I wake up from my dreams?
Why did I ever stop trying
　to make them a reality?

I want to make that little boy proud.
I want to find the hope he held on to
　when the world was crumbling
　　all around
　and he had no reason to believe,
　　but he did anyway.

I want to pick up the pieces
　my life fell into.

I want to keep trying
　to make the world a place we can be proud of,
　　where we listen
　　more than we talk over each other.

　Where we help each other up
　when we don't have the strength
　to stand on our own.

　Where we realize
　we can change ourselves
　if we don't like who we have become.

Someday,
I hope it all looks the way it does in my head.
  I know we can get there
  if we just listen a little more, instead.
I know it will take more than I know
  but I know now,
    those dreams are so much more
                than a show.

      I can't give them up.
      I won't let them go.

It's so beautiful, I see it —
just what we could be.

If I can do only one thing
  in the time I have left
  to live a life with no regret,

I hope it is this:

To leave behind a better world
than the one I came into.

I think underneath it all
  we are very much the same.

Flesh and bone and soul,
a desire to be happy and whole,
but often unsure of ourselves
                  or others,

      and trying
      each day
        to be better.

It is so important to try to understand
the things we do not,
the people we think we cannot.

Because all things deserve to be understood,
even the wicked and the cruel.

Sometimes they are just so
because nobody cares about them
or tries to understand
what makes them different.

You do not have to agree with someone
to listen to them,
to understand
the sadness in their bones
and the warm intentions of their heart.

This is a really good reminder — I needed this today.

Tomorrow Will Be a Good Day

I realize
I'm always living for the future me.

I endure pain now
  because eventually it will go away.
I am miserable now
  because eventually I won't be.
I do what I don't want to do
  so someday I can do
  what I *do* want to do.

I'm hoping someday
  it will all be worth it.

But when do I get to live for today?
  When do I get to live for me?

(Future me is so selfish.)

Let's go out tonight to a fancy
restaurant and live in the moment,
what do you say? (It's on me!)

It took me a while to learn how to say,
"I am not perfect
and that is okay."

It is okay to stumble along the way;
it is okay to not have all the answers some days.

I am not perfect,
but I am *enough*.

Yeah you are!!

SUMMER

Longevity

Sunlight cascades down grassy hills,
simmering the skin
and reaching deep inside the soul.
I feel a rekindled burning, a yearning
to blaze on now, from outside and within.

The long-awaited summer days
have finally come,
greeted by open, eagerly awaiting arms.

An unquenchable raw strength takes hold,
impossibly resilient and powerfully whole,
radiant and enveloping,
and steadily spreading, developing.
Young spring buds are now
full, deep roots, firm foundations,
built upon with continued strength.

Cool summer nights
spent splayed out on sweat-soaked backs,
staring up at stars that aren't our own.

And long, jubilant sunny days,
bright and blistering,
beneath our brightest light,
its gleam entrancing everything
with just a hint of magic and curious wonder,
all things new growing ever stronger.

These are the longest days, the furthest days
from the one where I had first begun.
I draw my strength from this summer sun,
enduring, enriched, and perspiring,
but trying with every breath to be inspiring.

I have spent so many moments,
too many days,
replaying all the battles I've fought
within myself,
with circumstances I wouldn't have thought
would ever come my way.

All this time
and I didn't stop to consider
the other people out there,
fighting the same battles too.

Maybe I could help them
put an end to the cycle.
Maybe they could help me,
if only we shared our stories
with each other.

Just think how beautiful this world could be.

I think you should — people need to know they
aren't alone and that other people — even
complete strangers — care about their well
being. ♡

It is so easy
    to get stuck where you started.

Where you grow up
    doesn't have to be where you settle down.

Who you were
    isn't who you have to be.

The things you have done,
    you don't have to keep doing.

You are in control,
    more control than you know.

Your days can escape from you
if you let them.

It is easy to fall into a routine,
to think of your dreams as too big —
too intimidating.

It is easy to find yourself
putting them off
and making excuses.

Doubt — uncertainty —
the part of yourself that says,
It is impossible,
can start to win you over.

But you are so much more capable
than you realize.
If there's even a small part of you
that says you can do it,
listen very carefully to it.

You can do **anything**.

Don't wait to live your life
or it will slip away from you.

If you want something more for yourself,
seek it out — pursue it —
now —
not tomorrow — **today.**

Self-Reminder #5

You don't have to be the strong one
all the time.

And whoever said tears were weak
never had the strength
to be vulnerable.

Sometimes facing your feelings is
the thing that requires the most
strength.

You

You are a *universe*
held in the cupped hands of yesterday.

You have the infinite possibilities of tomorrow
lingering in the shadows of your soul.

You can become whoever you wish to be,
you can lift yourself up on mountains,
you can sing from the tops of clouds,
you can write words of truth
that will be read for generations
upon generations,
you can do wondrous things
because you always have the word *now*
at your fingertips
and it allows you to do
anything –

if only you can find the courage.

୧/ଏ

I Am Here

I can't tell you how to feel,
    how to truly deal with your pain
        because only you know it
        as intimately as you do.

I can't tell you how to grieve,
    how to get up each day,
        despite the lump in your throat.

    How to build yourself up again
        when all you feel is broken.

But I can tell you
    I am here
    and you are enough.

    And I don't know if everything's
        going to be alright.

    But I can help you
        pick yourself back up.

    And I can walk with you
        if you want some company.

        Because it's a long road,
        but it's a little easier
        if you don't have to
        walk it alone.

Grief (Part 2)

It never really goes away

Some days, it gets really quiet and tidy
and folds up and tucks away nicely
in the back of your heart.

Other days, or in the middle of the night,
it's loud, and you can't make it quiet —
you realize the hamper is overflowing
and you haven't done laundry in a month.

The things you mourn become different.

The sadness sometimes becomes anger
or bitterness.

It doesn't always make sense
and it will upset you, how little sense it makes.

It doesn't get easier with time
like they say it does,
but it adapts, it changes,
it grows with you,
it forms wrinkles and crow's feet.

And when you've forgotten to call it in years,
it reminds you that it's still here.

What would you give
to know the stories I know?
To have learned the lessons I've learned?
To share the words of my heart?

Do you know
the scars I've collected to earn these?

Do you know
the pieces of myself I've lost?

Do you know all the things they've cost?

Please,
do not be so eager
to tread the same painful roads
        I have traveled,
to be who I am.

Please don't think this was a journey
I wanted to take.

Please don't glorify this pain.

Campfire

Write it all down.

All the words they told you,
all the weight you carried,
all the nights you cried yourself to sleep
or woke up and couldn't find the strength
to get out of bed,
all the bad memories you hold on to
because even though they hurt –
you're not ready to let go.

Bring them here.
We will sit crisscross around the campfire.
We'll watch the flames lick the air.

And we'll watch all the pain
burn away,
carried off by the wind.

Together

Rest.
There will be time again for waking
in the morning,
when the moonlight is fading,
when the healing has lifted you,
gracefully,
back onto your toes.

Then,
you can begin again.

Self-Reminder #6

When you're down on yourself,
I want you to look back
and remember all you've overcome.

I want you to massage your feet
because they've walked so many miles.

I want you to run your fingers over your scars
because they've survived so many battles.

I want you to look at yourself in the mirror
because you are here.

You've been dealt a lot
but you're here,
and that means something.

I want you to know
I'm proud of you.

I have heard the expression
treat others how you want to be treated,
but I've never had a problem with that.

I struggle instead with
treating myself as well as I treat others.

Yes! People like us always tend to value
others above ourselves.

Why do I hold myself to a higher standard
than what I expect from others?

Why do I tell myself
constantly
that I'm not good enough?

Why do I diminish the things I accomplish
when I should be proud?

If anyone else
talked about themselves
the way I do,
I wouldn't stand for it.

I need to start fighting for myself.

Same — I find this to be one of the
hardest things to work on.

Wise
Strong
Compassionate
Smart
Important
Genuine
Worthy
Hopeful
Inspiring
Kind
Happy
Interesting
Adaptable
Growing
Raw
Vulnerable
Tender

Enough
Always enough

Yes!!! This makes me so happy!!

Beacon

In my head, I was always the darkness.

But you lit something up within me,
a vibrant light
that formed from the pieces of myself
I believed were broken.

With you,
I am more than *treading water in the deep,*
wading through the shallows.

I can be a lighthouse,
a guiding light for those who are lost,
who are in the thick of the storm,
and want to see that there's hope
on the other side.

Thank you
for showing me the light within.

You've been a light for me more times than I
can count. ♡

Things I love about myself:

- I'm an extremely hopeful person, even when I have no reason to be

- I'm a good listener

- My blue eyes, full of wonder

- My kind heart

- The way I can make people laugh

- I'm always willing to learn new things

- That I've made strengths of my scars

- That I've given this strength to others

- How adaptable I have become

Self-Reminder #7

It's okay to ask for things,
as long as they're reasonable.

You deserve to be happy too.

You can let others take care of you —
you might be surprised
how much
they would like to be able to do that,

if you would let them.

Help me
find the people
who need to know
how much
we love them.

Stretch out your soul a little,
your body can hardly hold you in
but your heart is so full of love
and it's bursting at the seams.

Don't you hold it in,
not when you have
so much to give.

So much light to bring
to the darkness.

Don't let the pain harden your heart,
keep it soft like the clouds.

And give your flowers
room to blossom.

love freely and unashamedly ♡

Maybe you need permission
because some part of you
   doesn't feel like you deserve it
                   today.

But it's okay,
  you are allowed
          to be happy.

Begin again,
begin again,
begin again.
You'll see,
time will heal your deep-rooted wounds,
flowers will grow over your heart,
and love will find you again,
if your heart is open to it.

Never stop getting up,
never stop trying –
maybe today is the day.

Empathy

I feel your tears
running down my cheeks.

I hear the cracking, the splitting thunder
of your heartbreak.

I feel the weight of the expectations
they put on you,
the anxiety shaking your fingers.

I hear the words they've called you,
stinging, echoing, an ugly symphony
you listen to even when you close your eyes –
       the same words you've fallen asleep to
       and woken up to, as well,
         to find they haven't gone away.

I am sorry for all these things.
I understand the heaviness of getting up
       to start the day.

       Just know that I am here
       and we will be okay.

Thanks for being there for me yesterday.
♡

Dust

There is a dust
which sits atop distant memories

and it can't be brushed away,

only looked over — and through —

because the dust has become
a part of each memory itself.

We must accept
that it has become a thing of the past,

no matter how beautiful,
no matter how painful,
no matter how precious,
no matter how much
we want to simply
be able to wipe away the dust
and have it
as it was
so long ago.

I think there are little parts of ourselves
　　that we leave behind
　　　in all the things we love.

They are marked with us,
　　　changed forever
while we continue on,
sometimes revisiting
to leave a little bit more of ourselves
like lilacs or lilies,
　　　laid down beside a memory.

And maybe, for all we offer there,
　　we leave a little lighter,
　　with a spring in our step.

When my body begins to fall apart,
when I need new knees,
or maybe even a new heart,

I will try to have the wisdom
to know it is inevitable.

My body will ache
and my eyes will fail me.

But I will not let myself
grumble and groan
or become bitter and mean.

My heart will always
remain young,
full of love,
and wonder.

Our bodies weren't made to last
the length of our love.

Our souls will carry it up to the stars
in offering
when we crumble into dust.

To find the others like us,
the ones who loved,
the ones we lost,
and the dreams
we tied to balloons –
    distant echoes
    of what we would someday become.

This is quite beautiful ♡

My sweet father,
I hope I have made you proud,
I hope I have made you smile
amongst the stars,
I hope you still read my words
and send me your thoughts
on the wind,
I hope you will see us
walking here together,
and I hope
it makes your soul *sing*.

You live on in me.

Your ideas,
your tenderness,
your compassion –
         all the things
           that made you
               who you were.

I still feel them
    and so
        you are still here.

He does still live on in you and I love when we've been
able to do things to cherish that, like making the
recipes he used to cook for you. ♡

I want my son to know
I never figured out this world
and I don't think I ever will,
but if he wants to try
he can too.

Sometimes, things just don't work out
the way you expect them to,
but that's okay,
they work out
the way they're meant to.

He can be afraid
and cry
and never be ashamed.

Because he will know
I feel fear
and cry too.

When you're cold,
   I'll wrap my arms around you.
When you fall down,
   I'll help you back up again.
When your heart is broken,
   I'll show you how to put it back together.
When you feel alone,
   I'll watch the sun come up beside you.
When your eyes are filled with tears,
   I'll kiss them away.
When it feels like everyone has left you,
   I'll be here,
      walking with you
         into the darkness.

I don't know how I could be making it through this rough time if I didn't have you; thank you for being such a support, I appreciate you so much.

A Friend I Found Again

We were young and merry
when we met, our smiles resilient.

We shared starry skies with our eyes
and our dreams delighted us with hope
and wonder – of what could await us ahead.

We did the things that all teenagers do,
but we did it with an unbreakable bond
that ran deeper than whatever
we could find with others.

But one day a little crack began to form
and we poked and pulled and opened it up,
to draw our growing divide nice and wide.
We stared at each other from across the way
and we wondered how it got this far,
how we lost the words we used to say.

We spent days and nights in absolute silence,
wondering what the other was thinking,
wondering how to get back to before,
how to cross what we made
with our mistakes.

We got here, somehow, catching up again,
over a thousand miles apart,
sharing the same starry view we used to,
and making new memories for years to come.
Promising each other this unbreakable bond
will never again be undone.

A Poem for My Mother

For many moons,
we have danced beneath the starless skies,
we have traversed low roads,
through mucky ravines
and gotten our toes tangled in the bramble.

We came into this world fighting,
our teeth set, the odds against our survival.
We have a different breed of strength,
and our souls require a different forgiveness,
a kind we can only give ourselves.

We are wild and unforgiving,
and for a time, I'm afraid, we needed to be.
But we slowly became reckless and selfish,
guarded by walls only we could bring down
and in our lashing, we bit at each other.

I believe we have, at last,
some kindred understanding of each other,
as we realize we are still learning
how to live in our own bones
and how to reconcile with our footprints.

Dreams for Sale

For those who just can't anymore.

For the broken hearts
without the strength to heal.

For the hopeless –
whose hope was misplaced
and long forgotten.

For the ones who used to be strong
but found they could only be strong for so long.

For the empty and the lonely
who want to be overflowing with something –
anything at all.

I have dreams for sale.

There are so many
because you have left them behind
and I have collected them along the way.

They are here, for you,
if you want them back.

But if you do want these dreams again,
I ask only that you hold them close to you
as you once did –
with reverence
and awe and hope
and never let them go –
for they need these things to survive.

Thank You

Thank you for being my best friend.
Thank you for reading my words,
    even when they were hard to read,
    and seeing the hope buried between them.
Thank you for showing me
    the pieces of myself worth more than gold.
Thank you for trusting me.
Thank you for being you
    and for helping me rediscover myself.

I'm finally starting to see
what you like about me.

There's a lot to like, isn't there?

It always seems to be easier
for both of us to help each other
than to help ourselves.

Please
let me help you like you helped me,
let me show you the things you taught me,
let me be there for you
in ways you were there for me,
let me hold you as you held me.

Just because I've been through a lot
   doesn't mean you have to protect me
     from your own feelings.

   And it doesn't mean your feelings –
                your experiences –
     are any less important than mine.

Please,
don't push me away to protect me from you.
   I know that's what you're doing
     because I used to do that too.

I'm sorry I sometimes do this. It's funny how we traded places,
I'm in a darker place right now, but you're doing better. I guess
we balance each other out. Thank you for everything you do.
♡

There's something in the time
we spend together – some magic

that pushes all the darkness
out of my mind.

The songs,
the drives,
the late-night conversations.

You get me out of my own head.
You stay with me
when I shouldn't be left alone.

Thank you
for lying with me in the grass,
for making me feel normal.

It's dark out,
but in your eyes
I see fireflies
dancing in the night.

I love the connection we have, *unfiltered* *raw* time; it's
deeper than anything I've ever known. ♡

I See You

I see you now
   in a way I never saw you before.

I see you and my heart stops.

I see you and I remember what it was like
   to wake up Christmas morning as a child,
   with too much excitement to contain.

I see you and I forget how to speak –
   all the words I know how to say
                    have fallen away.

I see you and I see eyes that have known
   more pain than they should,
   but I see hope in them, too, and love.

I see you and I see how much you
   have lifted me up – how you've taught
   me to love myself.

I see you and I see strength,
   not in your body
   but in the way you carry it,
      in the way you go on
          despite what you've been through.

I see you and I wonder
   what you thought about wearing today –
   what you are thinking about now –
   what it feels like to be you.

I see you and I <u>really</u> see you
   and just you – without all these things
      the world piles on you.

  I see the beauty you hold inside.

I see you and I can't remember
   ever feeling this way before.

I see you and I can feel your fingers
   interlaced with mine.

  I feel your goosebumps
    ripple down your arms.

  I taste your lips against mine.

I see you and I wonder
   what colors we'll choose for our wedding.

  How many people will show?

  Will I feel as anxious as I do now,
      with all those people watching
    us watch each other –
      our love on display?

I see you and I feel the good days ahead,
   the days in the sun
      with our feet pushing into the sand.

   The cozy days at home with takeout
      and a book
      we take turns reading to each other.

I see you and I have hope
   for what the future could be.

I see you and I see our children's eyes,
   their cries as they come into the world.

   All the ways we care for them
   until they are old enough
   to care for themselves.

I see you and I see them growing
   too old to care about us,
      crooning over them.

I see you and I imagine
   what it will be like
   when we don't have to work anymore.

   When our bodies have caught up with us
   and all we have the strength left to do
      is sit across from each other
      and take turns reading.

I see you and I wonder
　　how I'll be able to get along
　　　　　　without you –
how I ever did before
and I remember that pain,
　　　　that loneliness that I'd forgotten about,
　　　　when I first saw you
　　　　　　all those years before.

And I feel that pain again
and it hurts worse,
　　worse than it ever did before.

　　Because now I know
　　　　what it's like to not be alone.

I see you and I know,
　　finally,

　　I'm home.

Oh darling, we've grown so much – I never expected our lives
to become intertwined the way they did, but I'm so grateful
they did, because with you, I'm home too. ♡ ♡

There will be tough days ahead.

I want to tell you that the worst
   is behind you,
      but who can really know?

I just know that there are always
                  reasons to smile.

         Even when my heart is broken,
            I'll find a way
               to make it love.

   And if you find you still need meaning,
      you need only listen
         to the silence,
      you need only feel
         the breeze on your fingertips.

      There is meaning for you here
               in all things.

Who will tell our stories
when the snow covers our bones,
when time wipes away the memory of us
from everyone's mind?

Will we be forgotten
when our grandchildren die?
Or maybe after our great-grandchildren?

Will our books still be read,
our love letters we wrote for each other,
will those be gathered up
and tucked in our caskets with us?

Or will we lie to ourselves
and say that they'll remember us
forever?

No More Favorites

Somewhere in our lives,
someone asked us our favorite color,
                        our favorite song,
                        our favorite movie,
                        our favorite food.

But I don't want to choose.
I don't want to be *just* one thing.
I am not one-dimensional.
            I want to be smart and kind *and* strong.

            Some days I want to cry.
            Some days I want to smile, to laugh.

            I want to love the beauty, the elegance,
            the vast depth of blue as I love
            the passion, the fire, the rawness of red.

It's okay to have an equal place in your heart
            for so many different things
            that are all important to you
                for different reasons.

            Please, don't think there's only room in
            yourself for one understanding.

It's easy to view others as one-dimensional sometimes, but
we are all so complex and one aspect of us doesn't define
who we are. ♡

There are so many sides to everything
and sometimes we get so focused on one
that we forget to appreciate the other.

I'm learning to appreciate the whole.

Long walks in the sunshine,
stargazing in the grass.

Blasting music you can dance to,
sitting in the silence,
with only your mind to listen to.

Ice cream cones at the beach,
snow angels and sledding,
spring flowers in blossom,
and the falling of the old
to make room for the new.

The new days ahead,
    the ones we wake to,
    we look forward to,
and the nostalgia of the old days –
                the good days
    the fond and tender memories
                we cherish forever.

        Who I was before,
        who I am going to be,
        and who I am *now*.

If

If you can grow flowers
  in a garden of weeds,
if you can smile
  when there are so many reasons to cry,
if you can dance shamelessly
  when it feels like everyone is watching,
if you can get rejected again and again
  and still get back up and keep on trying,
if you can look in the mirror
  and be proud of the person staring back at you,

if you can love yourself
  on your good days, as well as your bad ones,

then you've learned what it means
  to love yourself
          unconditionally.

It sure takes a lot to get to that point, I
imagine it feels worth it when you get there
though. ♡

I am so lucky
to be here.

I am so fortunate
to be alive.

I am so grateful
for *today*.

Maybe Today (Part IV)

Maybe today is the day
  I'm finally okay
     with where I am.

I'm seeing now that it's a beautiful place
  and it's taken me so long to say that,
  but now I can look in the mirror
   and not turn away in shame
         from my own face.

I no longer look over my shoulder
  at all the pain I was dragging
    for so many miles,
    for so many years,
because I've finally taken that backpack off.

And I don't know where it is,
  but it's somewhere back there
    where it belongs.

I no longer live my life swiping credit.
  I'm done making sacrifices
   to pave a better future
       for myself tomorrow.
I'm done neglecting my *today*.

I still have hopes and dreams,
   but they're no longer the only things
                I'm holding on to.

I'm done putting that pressure on them
   to make me happy,
   to make this all worth it.
I'm no longer telling myself
   maybe tomorrow will be easier,
   maybe tomorrow you'll get better.

   Why tomorrow and why not *today*?

Today is the day
   I keep putting one foot
                in front of the other
      and keep on going forward
                without looking back.

   I've been healing
      and I'm not going to stop.

No more maybes.
I can do this.
   I'm done making excuses.
   I'm done living everywhere in time
                except the present.

From now on,
         I'm living for today.

Epilogue

When I first began writing poems, I had no intention of any of them being read or being shared with anyone. I fled into poetry at a dark time in my life when I felt like I had all this anger and sadness and confusion pent up tightly inside me and it needed to find some release in a safe and harmless way.

There were many nights after my father died, after my mother tumbled down the hole of alcohol addiction, where I stayed up, scribbling away my thoughts and feelings by lamplight.

My words were always written from the heart, unyielding and unashamed – saying the things that my lips could never manage. Sometimes, those words were pathetic, or dark, or full of self-hate. And sometimes they were beautiful or hopeful. But they were always honest – because I never thought anyone was listening. Some days, or nights even after my life became more stable – I went back to writing again. Because I could always be honest with myself – I confided all my secret thoughts, my secret feelings.

But poetry, at least maybe mine, is meant to be shared. Even when it is difficult to do. Because out there, someone needs to read these words and realize that they are not alone, and what they feel, I feel it too. And that's okay.

– S. K. Williams

Acknowledgments

For too much of my life, I looked back at the dark corners of my past with sadness and anger. I used to feel so lonely, like no one understood what I was going through, and they never could. But looking back now, I see that I made it through the darkness because of so many people who, even when they didn't understand, did whatever they could to help make things better.

Thank you, Dad, for the impact you made, for being vulnerable and passionate, for always doing what was necessary and showing me hard work, for always making me feel loved, for igniting the passion for story, for adventure. You taught me the joy of a youthful soul.

Thank you, Mom, for showing me that people can change, for always encouraging me to grow and making me believe I was capable of anything, for owning up to your mistakes, and for getting back up after you fall. You taught me it's never too late to change who you are.

Thank you, Sabrina, for being a mother when I needed one, for supporting me in my passion, for always trying to understand me – even when it was hard to – for always being proud of me, for being a friend I could talk to any day, and for making sacrifices so that I could have a better life. You taught me to push myself, to fly at greater heights. To accept nothing less.

Thank you, Terry, for being a brother to me even before we were brothers, for asking me to be your best man when I didn't feel like I was the best at anything, for the special lime-green Game Boy you gave me in sixth grade when I was in the hospital, for always making me look at things in a different way, for being kind and understanding, and for showing me what it means to be a man. You taught me that I can be whoever I want to be in this world.

Thank you, Justin, for providing a home away from home to escape the chaos, for always being there for me, for your calls and your silly voicemails, for helping me feel normal, and for being unashamed in your passions. You taught me how to have fun and let go of the pressure.

Thank you, Stephen, for being a voice I could talk to in the dark, for our philosophical and spiritual conversations, for helping me not feel alone, for helping me through my worst, for stability and friendship, and for the special bond we share. You taught me to live my life for myself and to never look back with regret.

Most of all, thank you, Shayla. This whole book, this whole person that I am now, none of it even exists without you. You are everything. You taught me how to love myself.

Did you enjoy reading our story?

It continues in our first book, *Love by Night.*
Check it out if you want to read more about us.

Our next book comes out in the spring of 2024.

See you then.

You can also find more of our words on
Instagram and TikTok @skwilliamspoetry

Please feel free to write to us!